Wealth Building for Women

Empowering Financial Strategies

Table of Contents

Chapter 1. Introduction

In this empowering Special Report, we explore the vibrant and transformative world of wealth building specially crafted for women. Untangle the woolly metrosphere of financial strategies with a joyous sense of discovery, and unshackle yourself from any lingering monetary confines that have shadowed you in the past. Whether you're fresh in the workforce, forging a fiery path in entrepreneurship, or readying yourself for a golden, self-reliant retirement, these astutely curated strategies welcome women of all backgrounds and stages in life. Vividly written and teeming with empowering insights, "Wealth Building for Women: Empowering Financial Strategies" is the shimmering guide you never knew you needed! Get ready to embark on an enlightening journey that promises to bolster your financial acumen, shape your wealth-creating mind, and infuse you with unflagging confidence to become the architect of your abundant financial future.

Chapter 2. Sowing Seeds: Basics of Money and Wealth

Understanding wealth begins with understanding your relationship with money. The world might have instilled in you the belief that money is hard to come by or it only goes to those already rich. These beliefs, however untrue, can drastically impact your attitudes, behaviour and, ultimately, your wealth-building potential.

To forge a new path, to create a richer, more fulfilled life, you must first challenge and change your fundamental attitudes about money.

2.1. The Relationship Between Money and Wealth

When thinking about building wealth, it's crucial to distinguish between the terms 'money' and 'wealth.' Money is a medium of exchange, a tool that allows us to trade what we have for what we want. Wealth, on the other hand, is an abundance of assets that hold economic value. Wealth can consist of physical assets like lands or luxury possessions, but also intangibles like your ability to generate income.

Understanding this difference is the first step towards your own financial empowerment. Money is transient, while wealth can be grown, managed, and even passed on.

2.2. The Power of Financial Literacy

Financial literacy is key to your financial wellness. It's the knowledge necessary to make informed economic decisions. It affects your ability to save, invest, and plan for the future. By understanding financial concepts such as budgeting, investing, debt, inflation, compound interest, and taxes, you are better equipped to construct a wealth-building strategy unique to your circumstances.

2.3. Budgeting: Your Financial Compass

Even the journey of a thousand miles starts with a single step, and in our case, that first step is budgeting. By creating and adhering to a budget, you can prioritize your spending, save more effectively, and become aware of habits that may be hindering your wealth-building journey.

Tools like templates, apps, or old-fashioned pen and paper can help map out your spending. List your income, fixed costs (like rent or mortgage payments), variable costs (like utilities or groceries), and discretionary spending. Understanding where your money goes can give you the control needed to reshape your financial future.

2.4. Saving: Your Economy's Pillar

One of the most effective wealth building strategies is as simple as it sounds– save. A well-funded savings account not only gives you resilience in times of crisis, but it also allows you the chance to take advantage of investment opportunities as they arise.

Imagine setting aside a fixed percentage of income every month as part of your savings plan. Over time, this simple act can accumulate a significant amount of wealth, either as an emergency fund or as capital for future investments.

2.5. Investing: The Golden Goose

Investing takes your saving to the next level. It is the process of buying assets that provide a return over time, allowing your money to compound and grow. The key is to understand the different kinds of investments, their potential returns and their risks.

You can invest in stocks, bonds, mutual funds, real estate, businesses, and many other avenues. A diversified investment portfolio is not only a hedge against risk, but also a brilliant way to build long-term wealth. Start by understanding your risk tolerance, financial goals, and investment duration, then you can construct a tailored investment strategy.

2.6. Dealing With Debt

Borrowing money to meet your needs or wants is not inherently bad. However, uncontrolled debt is a fast ticket to financial ruin. It's important to consider the type of debt you hold – whether it's high interest credit card debt, a home loan, or student loan. Each has different implications for your wealth-building strategy.

Conquering your debt can be as simple as making a plan, sticking to it, and prioritizing high-interest debts. Debt can be a tool in wealth creation if it's used intelligently and judiciously.

2.7. Understanding Taxes

Taxes are a significant part of our financial landscape, and failing to understand them can lead to avoidable losses. By learning about different tax brackets, deductions, credits, and techniques for tax-efficient investing, you could save money and channel it into wealth-building efforts.

2.8. The Magic of Compound Interest

Albert Einstein famously called compound interest "the eighth wonder of the world." By re-investing your earnings, your wealth grows exponentially, not linearly. The sooner you start and the more you persist, the bigger the payoff in the end. Start investing small amounts early on in your working life, and let time do its magic.

2.9. Cultivating a Wealth Mindset

Finally, financial success goes beyond understanding concepts and crunching numbers. Cultivating a wealth mindset– the belief that you are capable of making, managing, and growing your money– can influence your financial longevity.

By investing in your financial education, adopting a mindset of prosperity, and taking practical steps to manage, save, and grow your money, you are already sowing the seeds for a prosperous future. Remember, wealth building is not a race against others but a personal journey towards financial independence.

Chapter 3. Cultivating Economic Power: Income, Saving, and Investing

Understanding the fundamentals of income, saving, and investing is integral in cultivating economic power. Embracing these concepts and applying them practically in your day-to-day financial management can pave the way for growing your wealth. Each section of this chapter will unpack these essential financial pillars, delineating the strategies you can employ to optimize your financial agency and power.

3.1. Understanding Income:

Income is the amount of money received during a period of time, usually in exchange for labor, goods, or services. Income is pivotal; it acts as the very cornerstone of wealth building.

There are various types of income:

- **Earned income:** The money you make by working for someone else or running a small business.

- **Unearned income:** Income received from sources other than employment, like investments or real estate rentals.

It's crucial to know the sources of your income and strategize how to maximize and diversify it. This could be through negotiating salaries, creating passive income streams, or leveraging side gigs.

3.2. Building an Emergency Fund:

One of the key tenets in personal finance is building an emergency fund. These are funds specifically set aside to cover large, unexpected expenses—such as job loss or a major health issue. A well-funded emergency reserve provides a safety buffer, giving you the ability to weather financial storms without going into debt.

A good rule of thumb is to have three to six months of living expenses in your emergency fund, accessible within a short time. Online savings accounts often work best for such purposes as they provide enough interest to keep your money from depreciating while still being easily accessible.

3.3. Budgeting:

Budgeting is a vital financial planning tool. It offers a clear view of your income, expenditure, and allows you to map your financial future. It's the best tool you have for managing your money, setting financial goals, and achieving them.

A simple budgeting plan could involve:

1. Calculating your income and expenses.
2. Setting your financial goals (these can be short, medium, or long-term).
3. Devising a plan to meet these goals.
4. Keeping track of your spending and income to ensure you're staying within your budget.

Budgeting postits disciplined money management and facilitates a robust savings strategy.

3.4. Saving:

The habit of saving primes your financial resilience. It provides the foundation for your wealth-building strategy. Strategies to inculcate a robust saving habit involve:

- **Automated savings:** Set up an automatic transfer from your checking account to your savings and investment accounts. This ensures you are consistently saving a part of your income.

- **High-yield savings accounts:** Consider opening a high-yield savings account that will allow your money to grow more rapidly via the power of compound interest.

3.5. Investing:

Investing represents a significant part of wealth building. It's the act of committing money or capital to an endeavour with the expectation of earning an additional income or profit.

Approaches to strategic investing include:

- **Diversification:** An investment strategy that recommends spreading your money across different investment types to reduce risk.

- **Long-term investments:** These are often less risky and have the potential for substantial returns over the long-haul.

- **Use of robo-advisors or financial advisors:** These tools or professionals can help navigate the investment landscape and develop an investment plan tailored to individual needs.

Remember, investing carries risks; it's important to do your research and consider seeking advice from a financial advisor.

3.6. Retirement Planning:

Retirement may feel far away, but it's never too early to start planning for it. Creating a robust plan and sticking to it ensures that you maintain your desired lifestyle in your golden years. Retirement plans like 401(k), Individual Retirement Accounts (IRAs), and other pension schemes are designed to grow your retirement corpus over the years.

When it comes to wealth building, remember that it's a gradually evolving, long-term process. Personal finance is personal—strategies that work for others, may not reap the same results for you. Your economic background, current financial status, and future goals all play a deciding role in your financial travel. The key lies in understanding the sacred trifecta of income, saving, and investing, and maneuvering them to your advantage. Nurture your financial knowledge, remain consistent, patient, and resolute, and watch the seeds of your economic power sprout and flourish.

Chapter 4. Charting Your Financial Waters: A Guide to Personal Budgeting

Navigating the vast ocean of personal finance may seem daunting, particularly when you're setting sail on your journey to wealth creation. Fear not, a well-crafted budget is the compass that will guide you through even the stormiest financial seas. It's more than just a ledger of income and expenses; it's the powerful tool that can help you thread the needle between current financial demands and future wealth aspirations.

4.1. Embrace the Power of Budgeting

Perceiving budgeting as a restrictive, joy-sapping exercise holds you back from realizing its true potential. Rather, envision this magnificent tool as an object of empowerment, a key to unlock the door leading to financial freedom. Beyond tracking your income and expenditure, it sprouts wings to your financial dreams, putting you in the driver's seat of your fiscal landscape and propelling you towards your goals.

Budgeting's far-fetched power lies wholly in clarity - offering a lucid view of your financial picture. Where are your earnings flowing? Are there unnecessary expenses shackling your potential savings? Is investment just a distant dream shrouded in a fog of uncertainty? Set up a budget and watch these mysteries unravel.

4.2. The Nitty-Gritty of Budgeting

To kick-start your budgeting voyage, gather about three months or more of financial data including your income, regular bills, discretionary expenses, and saving measures. This information builds the foundation of your budget.

Once you've assembled your data, it's time to put on your financial architect hat. Craft your budget around your needs, lifestyle, aspirations, and future expenditures. Here are the four major categories to focus on:

- Fixed Expenses: These encompass cost heads that remain relatively stable from one period to another such as rent, mortgage, utilities, groceries, broadband, and car payments.

- Variable Expenses: These are more spontaneous purchases like entertainment, shopping, travel which can fluctuate greatly.

- Investments: From mutual funds to stocks and bonds, account for all sources of investment. If you're just starting, plan an amount you would like to invest monthly.

- Savings: Building an emergency fund, saving for retirement, or any other purpose-specific saving falls under this umbrella.

4.3. Tailoring Your Budgeting Method

Unified as the underlying principle of budgeting may be, no single strategy fits all. The trick is to find the shoe that fits you best. Let's explore some of the more popular budgeting strategies:

- Envelope System: Divide cash for monthly expenses into physical envelopes — when an envelope empties, no more spending in that category until the next month.

- The 50/30/20 Rule: This strategy divvies up income into three broad categories — 50% for needs, 30% for wants, and 20% for savings or debt repayment.

- Zero-Based Budgeting: This method entails assigning every dollar of your income to a specific expense category, bringing the balance to zero at the end of the month.

- Values-Based Budgeting: This strategy involves prioritizing money allocation based on personal values such as travel, health, or education.

Each of these methods has pros and cons. The best-suited one depends on your lifestyle, financial goals, and personal preferences. Experiment and tweak till you achieve the perfect fit.

4.4. Ironing Out the Wrinkles

Any journey, including budgeting, might hit rough patches. Plans might come undone, financial mishaps may occur, but these are bumps on the road, not the end. They are opportunities to fortify your strategy, not an alarm to abandon the ship.

Crucial to remember is that budgeting isn't designed to be watertight. It ought to be a flexible document, accommodating unexpected alterations in your financial circumstances. Review and revise your budget monthly until you strike a harmonic balance.

4.5. Be Your Own Budgeting Pro

Learning the ropes of budgeting might seem like a steep learning curve at first. But, remember, every successful wealth builder was once a beginner. Just as drops make an ocean, small, consistent steps can culminate into a substantial nest egg.

Yes, managing one's finances can be tough. But with time,

perseverance, and a good budget, it's a code you can crack. With this guide on personal budgeting, you can navigate your financial journey with increased confidence and control. Map your journey, stand firm at the helm, and set sail towards a brilliant and bountiful financial future!

Chapter 5. Demystifying the Stock Market: Break the Glass Ceiling of Investing

Diving headfirst into the bustling and often overwhelming world of the stock market can be eye-opening, at least once you sift through the jargon and the numerical convolutions. Just remember, on the other side of the intricate matrix of data, there lies a universe of potential that is only waiting to be discovered.

5.1. Understanding the Market Basics

The stock market is a marketplace for securities, assets that represent an investment and can generate wealth. This wealth can be in the form of income derived from dividends, which are periodic payouts to shareholders, or capital gains, which is the increase in the stock price itself.

Imagine a fledgling company that needs money to expand. It could borrow by taking a loan, but paying back the loan with interest adds financial strain. Instead, it decides to issue stocks, which means the company is dividing itself into millions (or even billions) of pieces, or shares, and selling a portion of those shares to public investors. By buying shares, you become a partial owner of that company and are then entitled to a portion of the company's profits. This is the basic idea of investing in the stock market.

5.2. Rationalizing Risks and Returns

It's no secret that the stock market can be a risky business. Almost all investments involve some level of financial risk, the possibility that you could lose all or a portion of your money. However, risk and potential return are co-joined twins; the higher the potential return, the greater the risk.

For example, let's take two investment scenarios: a government bond and a high-tech start-up. The bond is considered a safe investment as it is backed by the government, but it returns a low interest. Conversely, the tech start-up could either skyrocket in value, providing exponential returns, or crash and burn, losing all your investment. This balance between risk and potential returns is a critical consideration in any investment decision.

To manage these risks, it's vital to diversify, or spread out your investments among various industries and asset types. If one sector takes a hit, your entire investment portfolio isn't brought to its knees. Instead, you're likely to have other investments that are performing well and can make up for any potential losses.

5.3. Choosing What to Invest In

There is a myriad of investment options in the stock market. Here's a brief primer:

1. **Individual Stocks:** Buying individual company stocks can be akin to a high-stakes game of poker. It offers the potential for high rewards, but at sizable risk. It's recommended for those who have a comfortable understanding of the company, the industry, and the market movement.

2. **Exchange-Traded Funds (ETFs):** ETFs are collections of stocks that track a specific index, like the S&P 500. They offer instant diversification, making them a good choice for novice investors.

3. **Mutual Funds:** They are similar to ETFs, but they're actively managed by a fund manager. This management usually comes at a higher cost, but may also result in better performance.

4. **Bonds:** When you buy a bond, you're essentially lending your money to a corporation or the government. Bonds are regarded as safer but return lower profits.

Since each of these asset classes fits different financial goals and risk tolerance, it's crucial to research and consider your investment choices carefully.

5.4. Devising Your Investment Strategy

Crafting an impeccable investment strategy involves aligning your financial goals, risk tolerance and investment timeline. If your goal is to save for retirement several decades away, you might choose to take on more risk in your investment portfolio because you have more time to recover from potential losses. On the other hand, if you're saving for a short-term goal, you may opt for less risky investments.

Next, you need to decide when and how you wish to invest. Dollar-cost averaging is a common investment strategy where you invest a particular amount of money at regular intervals. This method allows you to reduce the impact of volatility in the stock market and lower the risk of investing a large amount in a single investment at the wrong time.

Lastly, ensure to regularly review and rebalance your investment portfolio. Over time, some investments may outperform others, and your portfolio could become unbalanced. Regularly rebalancing ensures your portfolio continues to align with your investment goals.

Take heart, learning the ropes of the stock market might seem intimidating, but it becomes less daunting as you absorb more and more knowledge. It all starts with stepping forward into the arena. The world of investments is no more a men's playground; women, too, have begun to assert their financial prowess. Fazed by neither risks nor downturns, they are here to break the glass ceiling of investing, aiming for nothing less than the stars. Investing, for women, isn't just about money, it's about claiming their rightful piece of fiscal empowerment. Just remember, every expert investor was once a beginner who dared to take the first step into the unknown. And now, it's your turn.

Chapter 6. Entrepreneurial Ventures: Owning and Growing a Business

Entrepreneurship holds a unique appeal for many women, offering the possibility of financial independence, flexibility, and the opportunity to create and helm a venture based on one's passions. However, the path to successful entrepreneurship is paved with challenges and requires a focused blend of creativity, resilience, and strategic planning. This chapter will help equip you with the know-how to establish, nourish, and grow a profitable business.

6.1. Laying the Groundwork for Your Venture

To create a viable business from scratch, groundwork is essential. It encompasses everything from detailed market research to forming a clear vision for your entrepreneurial journey.

Market research is a critical first step. It helps you understand the existing market landscape, identify the target audience, their needs, and how your product or service can cater to them. Use a variety of research tools - surveys, interviews, online research - to gather data about potential customers and competitors.

Further, define your unique selling proposition (USP). It's what differentiates your product or service from the competition. Maybe your product is more affordable, has enhanced features, or stands out due to superior quality. Whatever it is, understand your USP and how to communicate it to your potential customers.

Develop a clear business plan. Include details about your business structure, an overview of the market, a thorough marketing strategy, and financial predictions. This plan will not only be a map guiding your activities, but it will also be imperative if you seek funding for your venture.

6.2. Understanding the Business Structure and Legal Aspects

Knowing the legal dimensions of your business is vital. It will protect your rights and your business. Here, we'll explore the most common types of business structures.

- Sole proprietorship: This is suitable for small businesses with one owner. It's straightforward to establish, but it leaves the owner personally responsible for business debts.

- Partnership: In a partnership, two or more people share ownership. Each partner contributes to the business and shares in the profits and losses.

- Corporation: This structure makes the business a separate legal entity from the owner, thus providing protection from personal liability.

- Limited Liability Company (LLC): This offers the benefits of both a corporation and a sole proprietorship. It provides legal protection without the strict regulations that corporations must follow.

Your choice depends on factors such as the business size, the level of control you want, and your capacity to manage risks.

6.3. Financing Your Venture

Having sorted the legal and strategic aspects, it's time to focus on financing your venture. Numerous options exist, from bootstrapping, bank loans, venture capital, crowdfunding, or even grants for women entrepreneurs.

Each method has its pros and cons, and the right choice will hinge on your specific business scenario. Regardless of the source, having a robust business plan is instrumental in securing funding.

6.4. Marketing Your Business

Now that you have your business idea, structure, and funding sorted, focus on branding and marketing. Your brand represents your business's identity and should communicate your USP. Invest in a quality logo, website, and marketing materials that echo your brand's message.

With a multitude of digital marketing techniques available today, it's easier than ever to reach your target audience. Social media marketing, search engine optimization (SEO), email newsletters, and pay-per-click (PPC) advertising are some strategies to learn about and employ.

6.5. Sustaining and Growing Your Business

Once your business is up and running, the challenge shifts to maintaining and scaling it. Monitoring your business performance with key performance indicators (KPIs) and financial metrics is crucial here.

Be open to evolving your product/service based on market feedback. Continuous learning and adaptability are the keys to the long-term success of any venture. Networking and building relationships with mentors and industry peers can also propel growth.

Entrepreneurship is a rich and rewarding journey that necessitates courage, persistence, and adaptability. As you venture into this exciting world, stay resolute and patient. The path may be demanding, but the rewards it brings — financial independence, personal growth, and the fulfilment of bringing your vision to life — are immense.

Iterating on and refining these strategies as per your specific situation will set the stage for a successful entrepreneurial venture. The power to create personal wealth through entrepreneurship lies within you – just strategize well, stay committed, and the path to financial wellness will open up!

Remember, every successful business once started as just an idea. Now that you have the roadmap, it's time to turn your idea into a successful venture!

Chapter 7. Navigating Real Estate: An Introduction to Property Investment

In life, few cities are devoid of bricks and mortar, be it cozy homes or towering skyscrapers. The real estate sector, colossal in its capacity, is an entrancing world full of potential riches. Understanding it is crucial for unlocking its value as an investment.

When we analyze any investment, the initial question invariably revolves around whether it's worth our time, effort, and of course, money. In the expansive universe of property investment, this question holds an even greater weight. With all its complexities and nuances, a lack of comprehension can spiral into lost opportunities and underutilized wealth.

7.1. Why Invest in Real Estate

You're likely aware that real estate spans beyond simply owning the roof over your head. Investors worldwide prize this sector for several compelling reasons.

Primarily, what sets real estate apart from other sectors is that it's a tangible asset that you can see, touch, improve, and directly control. As such, it offers advantages both practical, such as providing shelter, and financial, including asset appreciation and rental income.

Added to that, property is resilient. Even when markets get choppy, real estate tends to weather the storm more effectively than equities. Its fairly stable, predictable set of cash flows and potential capital appreciation provide a splendid solution to those with a distaste for the roller-coaster ride that the stock market sometimes embodies.

Moreover, tax advantages such as deductions related to property depreciation, mortgage interest, and necessary expenses can significantly enhance your overall return on investment.

Finally, real estate also offers the chance to diversify your investment portfolio, minimizing risks and optimizing returns. Alongside stocks, bonds, cash, and other assets, a rationally chosen property is a smart way to add some spice to a robust financial plan.

7.2. Property Investment Basics

Understanding the bare-bone basics of property investment is crucial before flirting with any actual acquisitions. While real estate is often dressed up in glossy brochures and enticing promises of rapid riches, caution should indeed accompany your enthusiasm.

Fundamentally, investment property is real estate that you buy with the intention of earning money, as opposed to living there. The most common methods of making money through property are by renting it and selling it for profit, also known as 'flipping.'

However, profitable property investment isn't simply about buying low and selling high or finding a tenant. It requires understanding the local property market, property management, running costs, taxation, legal obligations, and the vagaries of the real estate cycle.

7.3. Stepping into Property Asset Classes

On the surface, property may seem less complex than an enigma like the stock market, but beneath runs an undercurrent of vast diversity and choices. Like stocks are divided into technology, healthcare, manufacturing, and more, properties too are categorized into different types or 'asset classes.'

Residential: The asset class that most commonly springs to mind, residential property includes apartment complexes, townhouses, or houses.

Commercial: This asset class includes buildings used by businesses like offices, restaurants, malls, and others.

Industrial: Factories, warehouses, and similar assets fall within this category.

Retail: This class includes buildings like shopping centers and other stores.

Within each of these, further subcategories and niches exist, such as student housing in residential property and storage units in industrial property. And each of these asset classes carries its own investment implications, rewards, risks, and tactics.

7.4. Property Investment Strategies

The strategies to make money from real estate are as diverse as the landscape itself. They need to finely mesh with your individual investment goals, risk appetite, time, and resource commitments.

Buy and Hold: This involves buying a property and renting it out for a regular income stream and potential capital appreciation. This strategy is for the patient investors willing to withstand the fluctuating property market cycles.

Flipping (Buy, Renovate, Sell): Here, the property is purchased, renovated or upgraded, and sold for a profit. This suits those who enjoy tangible projects, understand real estate renovations, and know their local market inside out.

real estate investment trusts (REITs): This form of real estate investment involves buying shares of a company that owns income-generating real estate. It's effectively a way to invest in real estate without having physical ownership. This is most appropriate for those who prefer a hands-off approach and are comfortable with the volatility that equities can sometimes bring.

Among many other strategies, these are a few popular ones to get you started.

7.5. Wrapping Up

Investing in real estate can be incredibly rewarding, but it's not without its challenges or risks. Success depends on knowledge, critical analysis, and long-term commitment. Start building a solid foundation through self-education, market research, and financial discipline. Learn from property investing experts and join communities where you can exchange ideas and learn from others' experiences.

In the constellation of investments, property shines brightly. It's a living, breathing asset class, full of intricacies but also brimming with opportunities. Harnessing its potential could lead you to the wealth-building prowess you crave. The key is to proceed with wisdom, curiosity, and, above all, a vision for what you hope to achieve. The power to shape your financial future is in your hands.

Chapter 8. Saluting Retirement: Planning for Your Golden Years

Just as a captain meticulously orders every line and sail to chart the course of a ship, you, too, can foresee your voyage into retirement and prepare with similar attention to detail. Equipped with the right financial strategies and a visionary mindset, you can head into your golden years with confidence and prosperity.

8.1. Understanding Retirement

The first step towards financially empowering yourself for retirement is understanding what it entails. Retirement is not simply an age or period; it's a lifestyle change that can drastically transform your economic landscape. As your regular paychecks stop, your savings, investments, and pensions start to act as your income. The better you prepare, the smoother your transition will be into this new lifestyle.

Start by visualizing what your ideal retirement looks like. Whether you dream of owning a small cottage by the beach, relishing quiet moments with nature, or gallivanting around the globe in grand adventures, your dream retirement should be the anchor that grounds your financial strategies.

8.2. Assessing Your Financial Health

Once you have a vision of your retirement, it's essential to peep into your financial health. Begin by constructing a net worth statement listing all your assets (home, cars, savings, investments, etc.) and liabilities (mortgages, loans, credit card debts, etc.). Subtract your debt from your assets to establish a clear picture of your financial standing.

It may be a daunting task to see your financial life organized into cold, hard numbers. But clarity breeds control, and control is an essential ingredient of empowerment.

8.3. Crafting Your Retirement Plan

A robust retirement plan is like a patchwork quilt combining various components. Here are some of those foundational "patches":

1. Social Security Benefits: While it might not be the cornerstone of your retirement income, it still plays a critical role. Understand the process for claiming your benefits, and determine the optimum time to do so. Be aware that the longer you delay (up to age 70), the greater your monthly benefits will be.

2. Pensions: If you're fortunate enough to have a traditional pension plan, grab a solid understanding of your expected monthly payouts.

3. Savings & Investments: When it comes to retirement, time is on your side. The sooner you start saving, the more time your money has to grow. Ensure you harness power of compound interest by saving early and progressively.

4. Healthcare: Healthcare expenses typically rise during retirement. Ensure this reality doesn't surprise you by accounting for health insurance costs. Options like Medicare, long-term care insurance, and health savings accounts should be investigated thoroughly.

5. Taxes & Inflation: Develop strategies to minimize your tax burden, and remember that inflation will impact your purchasing power over time. Including conservative estimates within your plans can help align your retirement goals realistically.

8.4. Review Your Plan Regularly

One-time planning isn't enough. Your retirement plan, like any other financial plan, needs frequent reassessment. The shifting winds of life events, market fluctuations, or changes in retirement goals may necessitate recalibrations in your plan.

8.5. Securing Lifelong Income

Annuities can serve as dependable revenue streams in retirement, with the added benefit of lifetime income. With different types available (like fixed, variable, and fixed indexed annuities), conduct due diligence to understand their respective pros and cons.

8.6. Estate Planning

Estate planning involves determining how your assets will be distributed after your lifetime. Proper estate planning ensures your wealth passes to your loved ones according to your wishes, reducing their financial burdens and possible estate tax implications. Trust funds, wills, and beneficiary designations are key estate planning tools you might consider with advice from financial and legal experts.

As you set sail into your golden years, remember that the journey of retirement planning is intricate, just like any other voyage. It requires not only an anticipation of what lies over the horizon but also an appreciation of the current moment, fuelling the change with a mix of optimism and wisdom. Savor the power you hold in shaping your enriching future and let each step towards your golden years be a salute to the empowering self-reliant woman you are today!

Chapter 9. From Debts to Assets: Strategies to Minimize Borrowing and Maximize Saving

In our financial journey, we often oscillate between indebtedness and asset-building. This dynamic plays out in various forms: credit card debt, student loans, mortgages, car loans, and more. These financial obligations can loom large, casting long and imposing shadows over our financial lives, yet they also offer opportunities for growth, learning, and development. In this vital part of the guide, we delve into debt with a purpose: understanding it fully so we can formulate strategies to minimize its presence and impact, while maximizing your potential to accumulate wealth.

9.1. Debt Understanding and Management

Understanding debt is the first step towards managing it effectively. Debt is not inherently bad; it becomes problematic when it's improperly managed. Key elements are interest rates, payback periods, and penalties. Know your obligations intimately, scrutinize any hidden charges or fees, and understand the consequences of missing payments. Make it a habit to review and understand your credit statements. This knowledge will eliminate unwelcome surprises and provide a solid foundation for developing an effective debt management plan.

9.2. Developing A Debt Payment Strategy

Once you fully grasp your debt obligations, you can map out an effective payment strategy. The snowball and avalanche methods are two time-tested strategies.

The snowball method involves paying off debts in ascending order of amount, starting with the smallest, giving you quick wins that fuel motivation. On the other hand, the avalanche method prioritizes debts with the highest interest rates, curbing the accumulation of excessive interest.

Choose a method that resonates with your financial temperament and stick to it. The critical thing here is consistency. Even if you can only afford minimum payments initially, making regular payments imparts a sense of control and will eventually yield significant results.

9.3. Restructuring and Refinancing Debt

Sometimes, debt piles up to such an overwhelming extent that paying it off appears almost impossible. In such scenarios, debt restructuring or refinancing can provide some respite. Debt restructuring involves negotiating with creditors for reduced interest rates or extended payment terms. In contrast, refinancing involves taking a new loan to pay off existing ones, ideally with a lower interest rate or more flexible terms.

However, caution is necessary here. While these can provide temporary relief, they can also extend your financial obligations over a longer period. Carefully consider your options and consult a reliable financial advisor if you're unsure.

9.4. Emergency Fund Building

An emergency fund is your financial safety net. It can save you from resorting to borrowing in unexpected situations, and help in weathering financial storms without forfeiting important financial progress.

Start by saving small, consistent amounts in a unique, easily accessible, but separate account. Gradually build this fund until it can cover at least three to six months of living expenses. Notably, continue building this fund even as you pay off your debt. The reassurance of an emergency fund can reduce stress and provides a cushion should another financial obligation emerge unexpectedly.

9.5. Creating a Personal Savings Plan

Now that we've created a robust framework for managing and eliminating debt, let's shift focus to one of the most efficient wealth-building mechanisms: savings.

Begin with clear financial goals and then construct a personalized saving plan. Look to automate your savings; Technology has made it easier to do this with various apps and banking services offering automated fund transfers to savings accounts.

Your savings plan should embody SMART attributes: Specific, Measurable, Achievable, Relevant, and Time-bound. For instance, if you wish to buy a home, estimate the down payment needed, create a time-frame for raising the amount, and then determine how much you'll need to save monthly or weekly to reach that goal within the specified period.

9.6. Maximizing Savings

Expenses, like water, tend to find their level. To achieve savings goals, we must often become shrewd in managing our spending. Distinguish between wants and needs, prioritizing the latter. Living below your means will give you control over your financial circumstances, allowing you to save more effectively.

Explore opportunities for increasing your income. Overlook no possibility, small or large, ordinary or unique. Freelancing, part-time jobs, or even hobbies can significantly augment your income streams.

Lastly, consider the role of frugality in savings. Frugality doesn't mean deprivation or missing out, but rather wise management of resources.

9.7. Investing Your Savings

Savings kept idle can lose their value over time due to inflation. Educate yourself about various investment options like stocks, bonds, mutual funds, and real estate. Adopt an investment strategy aligned with your financial goals, risk appetite, and life stage.

As you navigate your investment journey, seek advice from professionals, and utilize reliable financial tools. Remember, the key is to start small and gradually expand your portfolio as you gain confidence and understanding.

In conclusion, the odyssey from debt to wealth building is filled with challenges, tests, and moments of self-doubt. But armed with the right knowledge, strategies, and a robust, unwavering commitment, you can navigate this pathway with astute financial aplomb. Learn to deploy debt wisely, to manage it with panache, and to transition, seamlessly and elegantly, from a life of indebtedness to a future of financial freedom and abundant wealth.

Chapter 10. Gatsby in Heels: Steps to Building Generational Wealth

Building generational wealth is not just about becoming rich or even wealthy, it's about securing financial stability for your future generations. It starts with creating and preserving wealth during your own lifetime, and then passing it on to the next generations in a way that enables them to build upon it. Now, let's start our journey through transforming financial landscapes.

10.1. Understanding Generational Wealth

Generational wealth, also known as family wealth or legacy wealth, is wealth that is passed down from one generation to another. This can include money, real estate, stock, or any other financial asset that provides a long-term impact on the financial security of your descendants. While building generational wealth might seem like a monumental task, it starts with taking the right steps today.

10.2. Step 1: Saving Multiple Streams of Income

Saving is the first and foremost step towards building generational wealth. However, savings must not be limited to the earnings from your primary job alone. It's vital to establish multiple streams of income - perhaps through a side job, investments, rental income, or a small business - and diligently save from them. Establish a saving goal and work steadily towards it.

10.3. Step 2: Investing Wisely and Patiently

Investing is different from saving. While savings safeguard fungible cash for short-term financial security, investing steadily grows wealth in the long haul and contributes significantly to generational wealth. The mantra is to invest wisely and patiently. Exchange-Traded Funds (ETFs), mutual funds, bonds, and stocks are some of the lucrative investment options. Real estate investment can also be a wise choice, given its relatively stable returns and potential for passive income.

10.4. Step 3: Purchasing Life Insurance

Contrary to popular belief, life insurance is not merely for the elderly. Purchasing a life insurance policy early not only guarantees financial security for your descendants in the event of your untimely death but can also function as a long-term investment vehicle. Whole life insurance policies build cash value that can be part of the wealth passed on to generations.

10.5. Step 4: Defining a Clear Estate Plan

An estate plan is more than just a will; it is a comprehensive blueprint for preserving and distributing wealth after your demise. It consists of wills, trusts, power of attorney, and beneficiary designations. A well-defined estate plan ensures that your wealth seamlessly trickles down to your descendants with minimal legal hurdles and tax implications.

10.6. Step 5: Building Strong Financial Education

Education is the most valuable asset you could bestow upon your descendants. It's crucial to inculcate strong financial habits in them as early as possible. Teaching them to save more than they spend, the importance of credit score, the art of investing, and the perils of debt can shape their financial acuity. Encourage them to read financial books, participate in financial education programs, or seek mentorship from financial experts.

10.7. Step 6: Creating Trust Funds

Trust funds are a tried-and-true tool for the preservation and distribution of wealth. Creating trust funds for your descendants not only provides them with financial stability but also ensures that the wealth allocated to them is used in a specific manner, as outlined in the terms of the trust.

10.8. Step 7: Investing in Real Estate

Real estate is a lucrative and tangible wealth-building vehicle. Investing in rental properties, for instance, can ensure a steady flow of income while simultaneously growing in value. Moreover, properties can be passed on to future generations, continuing the income flow and, potentially, growing with each passing generation.

10.9. Step 8: Minimizing Taxes

Generational wealth is not just about earning and accumulating wealth but also about preserving it from excessive taxes. Strategic financial planning, trust-fund creation, providing gifts, and availing of specific retirement benefits can minimize tax liabilities. Consulting a tax expert or financial advisor for this purpose is recommended.

10.10. Step 9: Constant Review and Update

Building generational wealth is an ongoing process that requires regular review and updates. Change in family structure, economic fluctuations, or updates in estate and tax laws may necessitate adjustments. Regularly evaluating your wealth generation strategy ensures it remains relevant and functional.

Creating generational wealth is a marathon, not a sprint. It demands perseverance, patience, and foresightedness. But with every step you take, remember, you're not just doing it for yourself, but for the future generations who would be standing on the wealth you have created, ready to create their own. By instilling those valuable financial lessons, steering clear from financial pitfalls, and consistently working on your defined strategy, you'll pave the path to financial freedom - for you, and the generations forthcoming. Your stiletto prints will be the roadmap they would joyously gallop through. Because when wealth meets wisdom, the Gatsby in you thrives.

Chapter 11. Being a Philanthropic Powerhouse: Giving Back and Shaping the World

You've heard the adage, 'We make a living by what we get, but we make a life by what we give.' There's profound truth in these words, especially when we're talking about building wealth. Possessing the power of wealth is not merely about hoarding or expanding one's assets; instead, it becomes truly meaningful when it is used to bring about a positive change - when it is shared and invested in making a difference. This chapter takes a fascinating dive into the art and science of philanthropy, the extraordinary potential of women as philanthropic powerhouses and how they can shape our world by giving back.

Chapter 12. Philanthropy: An Overview

Let's start with a brief understanding of what philanthropy really implies. Derived from the Greek words 'philos', meaning love, and 'anthropos', denoting humankind, philanthropy essentially symbolizes love for humanity. However, in today's context, it is not just about charity or giving handouts. It is about creating sustainable change, addressing the root causes of problems, and improving the quality of lives.

Chapter 13. Shift in Philanthropy: From Charitable Giving to Transformational Change

Historically, philanthropy has often been viewed as direct giving—donating funds to deserving individuals or organizations. While this is still pertinent, the philanthropy landscape is noticeably evolving. Now, we're seeing philanthropy imbued with clear focus, planning, and intent, aimed at bringing sustainable, transformational change.

Long-term approaches, such as impact investing and social entrepreneurship, are gaining ground. They ensure that wealth is distributed not just as a one-time gift, but as a continuous effort that fosters self-reliance and creates a broader societal impact. Here, the wealth creator takes on the mantle of a changemaker, prudently guiding their assets to generate both financial and social returns.

Chapter 14. Women in Philanthropy: The Game Changers

Fast-emerging as philanthropic powerhouses, women are injecting fresh impetus into the traditionally male-dominated sphere. Their approach towards giving is distinctive: it is sensitive, thoughtful, inclusive, collaborative, and often directed towards causes affecting women and children. Not only do they donate from their personal wealth, but they also encourage community involvement and create influential social and philanthropic networks.

Whether they're heiresses, entrepreneurs, or professionals, women are increasingly gaining control over significant resources and are channelizing them to important causes. This ascending influence of women in philanthropy is a global trend that's heralding an age of 'feminine capital'—an exciting shift carrying the potential to revolutionize the landscape of giving.

Chapter 15. Philanthropy within Your Reach: Breaking Stereotypes

You might wonder, 'Does philanthropy require immense wealth?' If you are thinking semantically, you'd be correct in believing so. However, an essence of philanthropy, its soul, lies in everyday acts of kindness and generosity. It is about giving—giving with compassion, giving strategically, and giving your time, resources, expertise, or skills for the well-being of others.

Microdonations or crowd-funded initiatives can cumulatively add up to significant contributions, proving that it's not always about 'how much' but 'how'. You could volunteer your time and skills to mentor a startup, contribute intellectually to a project, or use your professional expertise in a non-profit, proving that philanthropy can take various forms other than just monetary.

Chapter 16. Becoming a Philanthropic Powerhouse: How?

As you embark on this altruistic journey, the first steps involve identifying your values and passions. What matters the most to you? What kind of societal change are you aspiring to create? Essentially, philanthropy should resonate with the giver's personal ethos.

Next, devise a strategic philanthropy plan. Just like financial planning, philanthropy also demands due diligence, clarity, and a well-thought-out strategy.

Moreover, consider the 'giving while living' approach. This concept, popularized by Chuck Feeney, advocates for the immediate and thoughtful use of personal wealth for creating an impact, thereby allowing you to witness the fruits of your giving during your lifetime.

16.1. Engage, Educate, and Empower

Practicing philanthropy arm-in-arm with the principles of engagement, education, and empowerment can create a far-reaching impact. Engage with the cause, the community, and stakeholders. Educate yourself on the issues you are passionate about and empower others by sharing resources, time, and skills, shaping a world of equal opportunities.

Chapter 17. Successful Women Philanthropists: Learn from Their Journeys

Stories of women philanthropists, such as Melinda Gates, Priscilla Chan, and Laurene Powell Jobs, are awe-inspiring. They're not just writing checks but are actively involved in their chosen causes, collaborating with various organizations, advocating policy changes, and striving to create sustainable solutions to pressing global issues.

Chapter 18. Conclusion: Embark on Your Philanthropy Journey

Irrespective of the size of your wealth, you can influence and shape our world positively. By strategically utilizing your resources—financial, intellectual, or temporal—you can make a difference. As a woman stepping into the world of philanthropy, you have a unique perspective and an instinctive desire to foster change.

Remember to plan, research, engage, and evolve on this enriching journey. Strategize your philanthropic efforts and align them with your long-term financial goals. Ultimately, the joy derived from making meaningful contributions and shaping a better world is indeed priceless. After all, it's not just about being wealthy—it's about being wealthy and wise. Push beyond the realms of wealth accumulation and embark on the generous journey of philanthropy, for in giving, you receive.

www.ingramcontent.com/pod-product-compliance
Lightning Source LLC
Chambersburg PA
CBHW071006260726